# STEP LIGHTLY

*poems by*

# Donna Wolf-Palacio

*Finishing Line Press*
Georgetown, Kentucky

# STEP LIGHTLY

Copyright © 2017 by Donna Wolf-Palacio
ISBN 978-1-63534-346-5 First Edition
All rights reserved under International and Pan-American Copyright Conventions.
No part of this book may be reproduced in any manner whatsoever without written permission from the publisher, except in the case of brief quotations embodied in critical articles and reviews.

## ACKNOWLEDGMENTS

With thanks to my wonderful family and friends.

Publisher: Leah Maines

Editor: Christen Kincaid

Cover Art: Reynaldo T. Palacio

Author Photo: Christine M. Palacio

Cover Design: Elizabeth Maines McCleavy

Printed in the USA on acid-free paper.
Order online: www.finishinglinepress.com
also available on amazon.com

Author inquiries and mail orders:
Finishing Line Press
P. O. Box 1626
Georgetown, Kentucky 40324
U. S. A.

# Table of Contents

Camels ............................................................................. 1
Mask ................................................................................ 2
Beirut .............................................................................. 3
Vermont ........................................................................... 4
When I Was Young ........................................................ 5
Hells and Hierarchies ................................................... 6
Late July ......................................................................... 7
Furniture ........................................................................ 8
Chicken Little ................................................................ 9
Scholar .......................................................................... 10
Two if by Sea ................................................................ 11
Step Lightly .................................................................. 12
Consider Spring ........................................................... 13
New York ...................................................................... 14
News from the Frontier .............................................. 15
The Modern Believer .................................................. 16
The Clock ..................................................................... 17
Most of the Time ......................................................... 18
Self-Portrait ................................................................. 19
The Moon Fell Down the Stairs ................................ 20
Object: Photograph of a Horse in a Field ............... 21
Collateral Damage ...................................................... 22
Evening - Spring ......................................................... 23
The Other Glove ......................................................... 24
The Point ...................................................................... 25
Art Exhibit on Lancaster Avenue ............................. 26
She Walks Alone ......................................................... 27

**Camels**


If there is a way to multiply their stride
and lift their heads out of the desert,
this is what they intend to do.

Without language, they rely on what they see,
and the wind.  Their weighty humps, their noses in the air,
their soft fur barely visible.  They are the well-steered songs
that plod across my sleep.

While I, in that ancient factory,
look for clues and artifacts.

**Mask**

Here is the chicken.  Here is the bread.
Are you happy now?
Do you want another body?

When is it time to buy flowers?
Or plant them? Or eat them?
Or are they always new, unbroken by memory?

Do you still leap for the right word?
Do words appear, or are they summoned?

If the world shatters will you pick me up and hold me to your ear?
Don't lie, remember how folding leaves dance paper dances
behind masks that frighten children out of darkness.

**Beirut**

Wouldn't you like to meet the moon
and float with it into the winter sky?
Where else can we rest?

Night comes.  We conjure phrases
we have practiced, feed them,
to the hopeful that pray at the door.

The voice that fills this narrow cave
seems timid, sweet.
But its time has been up
since birds flew against the windows.

Yet the voice still calls.
We dance a fierce dance, pound the stone floor,
till we wake or the dead hear us.

**Vermont**

No fences here, no train
to take me out on.
I stumble past cow and horse, ponies who wave
their heads and bow, a plain
wood house.  By a shaded stream
I watch till the stones move.

**When I Was Young**

I stood every spring by the spruce near the driveway,
breathing it in, planning for unscarred explosions, hairy stems,
and purple lilacs that burst against the wall.

I stored all the rage in the closet,
torn shirts, frayed notebooks, mountain of boxes of ice skates and albums,
secret trap door in its corner.

In dreams, birds whistled, had heads like plates.
Their feathers opened like the spaces
between my fingers. Their wings were rough
as tribal blankets.

In the kitchen, with my nail, I scratched the white varnish
off the counter, peeled it to the hard black surface.

These things I did to wish the sun alive.

Years later, I cover my eyes, see shapes through gauze.
Ron sings in his sleep. Down the hill, the river
moves through green skin. Diamond waves
unfold near the bones of an old bridge.
They move, and moving live their secret.

## Hells and Hierarchies

> *"All hells and hierarchies are works of the imagination."*
> *Anthony Madrid*

Could it be more true?
The past
a plate
we can't break.
Each piece has
a spot.
And there it is, outlay to the outlay.
Mind around it
in memory. The stone falls.
Maybe a small stone.
Still, a stone.

**Late July**

Some days, it seems
the sky pushes through
to tell me one true thing.
But I have no intention
of being pulled in
by belief or wonder.
Sometimes, I regret this.
I go ahead, make a sandwich,
watch the most devastating news
and feel my voice drowned out
by bombs and rationalizations.
This is past imagination.

All of it is so the same, we'd be better off
without words.
Then I would eat your food,
and you would eat mine.

But that's fading, and no plausible world is in sight.

**Furniture**

In my dream my father
was selling the house on Garden Road.
People came
to look at the washing machine and the furniture.
I was in my robe, not prepared, still getting over my shock
that he was still alive. The desks, chairs, and tables
were old and worn. I knew
he would take any offer. I knew
it was still his house, and I couldn't have him
declared incompetent
since he'd done such a good job
of calling prospective buyers.
I was sad about losing the yard,
but I figured that would be the last to go.

**Chicken Little**

Better to believe in something you can spare.
Not religion, of course, but a butterfly would be nice.
You can hold it and let it go.  Butterflies don't see
our arbitrary fences, our attempts to name beauty.

At six, I read my first book, "Chicken Little".
I was so proud of myself.
"The sky is falling" meant something and nothing to me.

Little did I know.

**Scholar**

The sea is vast, the shore unreachable.
My reach is short, outstretched, unfinished.
On the beach, the ocean
turns clear for a moment
in crests that filter the sun
and give the waves the illusion of power,
though they are just hands falling
after the arm.

## Two if by Sea

1
Today, a man of no inspiring grace stands on a ship.
The visor of his cap covers his eyes.
This man is the emperor of big.

2
In 1775, a man on a horse says to his friend, "One if by land,
two if by sea", points to the belfry arch of the North Church tower.
He silently rows to the Charlestown shore.

Hovering, phantom ship, huge black hulk, magnified
by its reflection in the tide.
His friend climbs the wooden stairs of the tower.

The man on the opposite side
sees two lamps in the North Church tower,
mounts his horse, rides through village and farm
to Lexington and Concord.

3
So who is who and what is what?
Can the Mystic River foresee the dimming of the light
and how it will rise in that land of mountains?

**Step Lightly**

You never seemed to get it right, the puzzle of your mother.
No god or therapy could free you from those wires she tugged
to keep the medicine flowing. So you read the masters for a sign,
Winnicott, Freud, the family people, stars so far away,
yet windows of hope for a real eternity.

Some days I see your eyes blink with disbelief
at their humane unwavering light.
Yet while you searched, your words and teaching
brought you to the source. Sometimes, you couldn't take it in.
There was so much rage in you. But other times you took it whole,
and what you made was personal, irreplaceable.

## Consider Spring

Sometimes, driving past my childhood home,
I feel my heart is breaking.
When my brother died eight years ago,
we asked for a sign. One azalea bloomed
through November.

Death isn't only what we think,
darkness and disintegration,
but also the loneliness and rebirth that come after, stay with you,
blossom even in the wrong season.

It has its own county, this sadness, like mind,
thin empty branches arranged in an order
we can only guess is there to guide us.

It's a country of turning-to-color,
of roses, hydrangeas, and pines, of the past
flooding the future, while we catch our breath
to let it invade our bodies.

# New York

Runners' shadows slide across panes, their final race.
A laughing statue traps a grin on the house across the street.
It finds in its animal mask a face it can endure,
while my face watches, grows softer, grows older.

If you get bolder, memory will pin you down in dreams,
and you will meet yourself in spite of what you thought was intractable.
Face facts, the universe must meet itself somewhere.
No snapping back is predicted.

A star that faces other stars will slowly move the other stars aside.
Scientists are sure the universe is spreading, and far away is just a notion,
a sweet concoction. Why did we think

pure abstraction could ever be held like a penny or a slate,
written on or not, erasable or not? Let's face it, we are not ourselves
without the trace of what has gone before. The least attempt at persuasion
convinces us that time is wrapped in itself,

a wide ribbon or scattered shore
that can't remain for long, although perhaps
it has been here all along, practicing.

**News from the Frontier**

This may not be Chang'an, the mountain city,
and I may not see from here the blue hills recede into darkness.
I listen to crickets vying for dominance over summer birds
and winning. The supermarket begonias cluster with the country geraniums,
and the fresh mint hides on the outside of the wooden planter.
People march past waving their hats, if they have hats,
and holding up their happy babies.

How long have I been writing this poem?
It seems like minutes, but it is more like years.

## The Modern Believer

must constantly guard his beliefs against doubts.
Pascal saw this, and Kierkegaard, so philosophy has always had a slight edge
over religion.

Without authority, no permanence, no reliability?

Have we ceased to live in a common world?
Which will we choose, the pyramid? The onion?

Our hearts may be in the right place, but our minds wander
between the notion we are living in a modern world
and our clutch around tradition
down to the flavors and colors that love us,
the way bees love nectar, immersed and thirsty.

## The Clock

Seven is a bird with a broken wing.
Two is a man running.

I have made many mistakes in my life.
Soon the house will be filled with going.

I want to get up, stand up.

I couldn't wake you.  I knew you were breathing
from the rise and fall of your body.
I tried to make a plan, but none of it made sense.

You woke up.  You are afraid.
We are always skimming the surface of fear.
It's not just what you do for me,
making sense of our lives,
but the thousand filaments that tie us together.
I miss what we lose.

On the Chinese clock,
seven is a bird with a broken wing.
Two is a man running.

## Most of the Time

I am in time, and time is in me. Then suddenly
these digits elude me. I think they are not moving forward.
In a moment, I correct for it, bring them back to earth.

Today is the anniversary of the expansion. Well, every day.
It shuffled off its stars on a day like today.

Each day parades as the fulfillment of a dream,
a wish, a longing. Each day is a ghost
and an embodiment.

Pretend I'm lifting you to pick an apple off a tree you can't see.
You take my word for it, and the apple appears.

When we got the call
that my brother crashed into a tree,
I went down to the deck and bleached the table white.
It was three in the morning. My hands wanted something to do,
waiting for the sun.

Do you really want to know what is out there?
Who will you take for company?
Who will console you?

**Self-Portrait**


The weather breaks, sun appears.
Good intentions.
The ant lifts his arms
to the soft pink blossoms.
He can't tell which are dead, dying,
or in full bloom.  On the other hand,
if he's lucky,
no one stops him at the border.

## The Moon Fell Down the Stairs

Everything is covered with dust,
say the wise ones, but they mean later, not now.
The paintings of the virgin are like unopened pecans
on a plate near rosy fruit, their skin slightly hazy
and gold in the indoor light
of a parlor or whatever fuss they made
over the green-blue oriental cloth, with fringes,
thrown over the heavy wooden table,
fringes gold as fire.

**Object: A Photograph of a Horse in a Field**

On the wall, horse in a pale green mist.
Curtain of leaves in the morning light, a thin red road.
The light moves, leaves its track upon the grass.
The mist, the fence, the horse.
They find their way, hidden pebbles in a lake.
It is full, this light, for its own sake.

## Collateral Damage

What has become of Kant or Hillel on one leg?
That twist of hate we recognize never disappears.
So  bombs, like Icarus, fall.  Auden knew:
*while someone else is eating or opening a window or just walking dully along...*
Can you erase the past
with something that falls from the sky?

**Evening – Spring**

Quiet night.  Body humped like a cloud.
Dreamy air turned to a coarse grey castle
raising and lowering its bridge.
This is the wage of wandering apart from the castle,
into the green field, where lying still takes the unquiet body
out of itself.  We rise on a blue ladder.
We are flooded with light.

## The Other Glove

Do you see that glove on the table?
In this house is its twin.
The past of the past flips back.
We used to know how much to lie
to keep up with the truth.

Families are like that.  You can't remember
how you got where you are, but you know
you hold a bigger truth, a mountain worth climbing.

In breath/out of breath.  Nothing matters but the climb.
There were times, I swear, we made it.
If one stepped back, the other stepped forward.
Then one day we couldn't keep the honesty at bay.
We were both so tired.
It is hard to accept the collapse of the body.

**The Point**
*for Ron*


Every time I'm up at night, you're already awake
as if some other eye has caught you in its blurry net
and you can see no further use for sleep.

You master all the imperfections of the house
in ways I never could.  With you here,
the roof won't fall.

But where, when I am swimming blind,
in a place I fear to see,
will I look for you, or wait for you to find me?

## Art Exhibit on Lancaster Avenue

James Joyce all chopped up.
The netting in the reflection was a stroke of genius,
the hanging pot-like discs. I would have loved to hear the words.

**She Walks Alone**

past the old tree wires on branches,
dreamy shadows, blue pots on windowsills..
The few leaves not yet retrieved.

How pointless to imitate nature.
Meaning and pattern are not the same.
While the wind moves through the trees,
mind crushes ideas in a great crusher,
but the wind, still blind, breaks free.

Donna Wolf-Palacio's books of poetry, *What I Don't Know* and *The Other Side* were published by Finishing Line Press. She received an MFA in Poetry from Columbia University's School of the Arts. She has published in *Poetry, The Pennsylvania Gazette, Voices, The Musehouse Journal, Intro, The Interpreter,* and *Writing from the Heart: Poems about Adoption.* She wrote a collection of versions of Chinese poems, "The Heart of the Dragon". She has taught a poetry workshop at the University of the Arts in Philadelphia and was editor/consultant for the UARTS Poetry Review.

She has done many readings and workshops in New York and Philadelphia. She has received grants and fellowships from The Leeway Foundation, the National Endowment for the Humanities, the University of Pennsylvania, Columbia University, New York University, Bryn Mawr College, the Psychoanalytic Center of Philadelphia, the Postgraduate Institute of New York, and the Pennsylvania Council of the Arts. She is a psychotherapist who lives in Philadelphia with her husband and daughter.

www.ingramcontent.com/pod-product-compliance
Lightning Source LLC
LaVergne TN
LVHW041517070426
835507LV00012B/1626